Mastering Sales Language

Eliminate These 21 Harmful Phrases
& Embrace Words That Sell!

Brian K McNeill

Empowerment Publishing & Multi-Media

Mastering Sales Language

Eliminate These 21 Harmful Phrases & Embrace Words That Sell!

Contact admin@epublishyou.com for bulk orders or brian@briankmcneill.com for more information on speaking opportunities.

ISBN- 9798329920611

Table of Contents

Preface...iii
Introduction......................................vi
Chapter 1: Let Go of Limiting Beliefs.........1
Chapter 2: Value and Communication.........3
Chapter 3: Customer-Centric Approach........5
Chapter 4: Financial Assumptions.............7
Chapter 5: Leads and Communication.........9
Chapter 6: Building Confidence...............11
Chapter 7: Self-Belief and Selling............13
Chapter 8: Words to Avoid in
Sales...15
Chapter 9: Keywords to Use Much More
Often...21
About the Author..............................31
Bibliography...................................34

Preface

I once heard of an experiment conducted by a school system. Before the new school year began, three teachers were called in and informed that their unique skills as educators and leaders had not gone unnoticed. Because of their obvious effectiveness, they were rewarded with 30 particularly bright children each for the upcoming year. They were told that the students in their classes would be the best and brightest.

Sure enough, the teachers and students had an incredible school year! The teachers loved and enjoyed their students more than ever before, and the students excelled in every metric. It was a wonderfully successful year for everyone involved.

When the school year ended, the same three teachers were called back into the office. They were asked how they enjoyed the school year, and they could hardly stop bragging and feeling wonderful about what they had accomplished.

Then, the administrators revealed a secret: they had chosen all of the children at random. There was nothing particularly special about any of the students. The teachers, still riding high on the success of the year, realized that even with randomly selected students, they succeeded because of how good they were at teaching.

Then came the next revelation: the administrators had actually selected the teachers by picking their names out of a hat.

Wow! If this were true, then why did they have such a successful year?

Could it be because of a thought they accepted? Could it be because someone said something positive about them, and they believed it, leading them to perform to that level of expectation?

I submit that this is exactly why!

However, the converse is also true. The thoughts we accept about selling and business greatly impact how well we perform. Join us on a journey through this book, where we will uncover and conquer the limiting beliefs that entrepreneurs, businesspeople, and salespeople must let go of right now!

Introduction

In the world of entrepreneurship, success often hinges on effective sales strategies. However, the journey to sales excellence is frequently impeded by the words we speak, not just to others but also to ourselves. What we say shapes our subconscious mind and influences our actions.

This book delves into the 21 things that entrepreneurs should stop saying – even to themselves – to pave the way for sales success. It also covers how certain words used during the sales process can make or break your success and provides alternatives to enhance your communication with potential clients.

Chapter 1: Let Go of Limiting Beliefs

1. I'm not a salesperson
Let go of this limiting belief. There really is no way of getting around this. If you are an entrepreneur, you are in sales. Everyone can improve their ability to sell, even you.

2. I don't like selling
Shift your mindset; embrace selling as a means of helping others. Do you like getting money in exchange for something that you offered? Of course, you do. You like a sale being made, but you don't like the potential for rejection and not understanding how. You can learn.

3. I don't have to sell; if they want it, they'll buy it
Don't leave your success to chance. Actively promote what you offer. If you are an entrepreneur, yes, you do need to sell. If you want to keep on doing your passion work, you will have to sell.

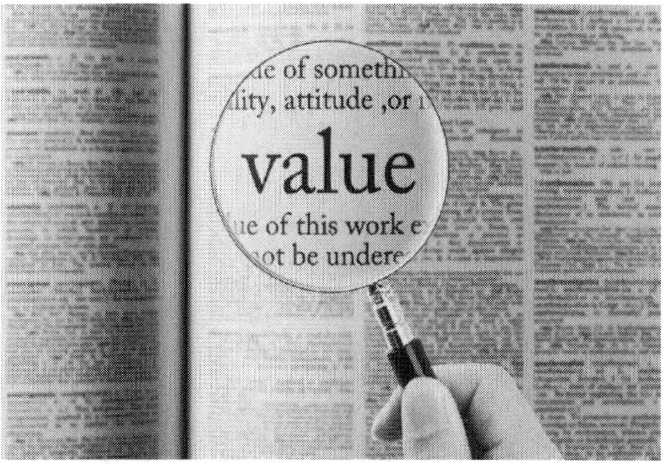

Chapter 2: Value and Communication

4. No one can afford me
Value your offerings and communicate their worth confidently. This is simply not true. At any given moment, people are paying significantly more for what you are offering from someone else.

5. My branding and website will sell for me
Your online presence can support your sales efforts, but you must be the driving force behind the sales process. Your branding and website can position you into a place where you can sell. Branding and web presence are essential, but you still have to ask for the business.

6. My social media will sell for me
Social media can create awareness, but it's your job to close deals. This is particularly insidious because the idea is so fun and so romantic. Again, social media only helps put you in a position where you can sell. It will not do your work for you!

Chapter 3: Customer-Centric Approach

7. Salespeople are pushy
Dispel this myth and embrace a customer-centric approach to selling. This ideology needs to go the way of the dinosaur. Have you seen a pushy salesperson in years? No one today can get away with selling like this, and no one even tries this method anymore.

8. I hate closing
Instead, focus on creating value and helping your customers reach the decision to buy. You simply do not know how to close, but you can learn.

9. My pitch

Shift from a rehearsed pitch to a natural conversation. I believe the whole concept of pitching is passé. Do not pitch! Tell your story.

Chapter 4: Financial Assumptions

10. Pitching
Engage in genuine discussions rather than relying on pitches. Does this word feel good to you to say? Stop saying it.

11. Nobody has any money
Don't prejudge your potential customers' financial situation. Try parking at any mall during any holiday season. The parking lots are full of people with the money to buy what they "want." You can help them to want what you offer.

12. If they don't buy it the first time, I leave them alone. Persistence can lead to sales. Follow up with prospects who show interest. Have you ever gone on a date with someone that you initially said no to? Exactly.

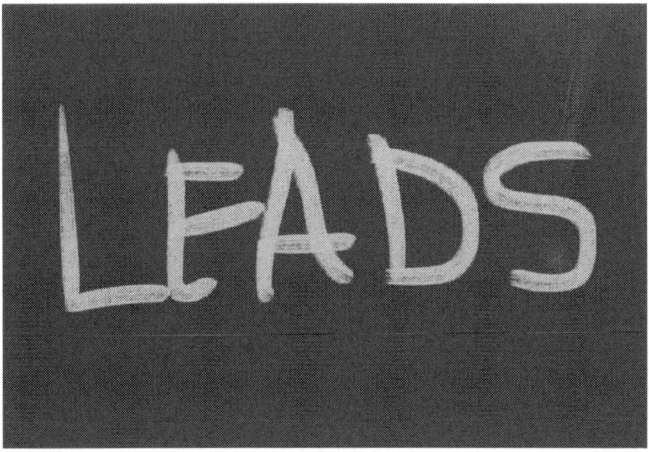

Chapter 5: Leads and Communication

13. I've got tons of leads
Quality over quantity; focus on converting leads into customers. Leads do not equal sales! Converting leads into sales equals sales. Selling is a process.

14. They don't understand
Improve your communication skills to bridge the understanding gap. Make it simpler to understand and cut out jargon!

15. Anything negative about a potential client
Maintain a positive outlook in all interactions. It will get back to them. Also, the air is different when you are not thinking positively about your potential clients.

Chapter 6: Building Confidence

16. I'm not good at selling
Build your selling skills over time through learning and practice. Selling is a skill that can and should be learned.

17. Anything negative about people that sell
Avoid negative stereotypes about salespeople; they can be valuable allies. Your subconscious mind will not allow you to do anything well that you find distasteful. They are amongst the best-informed and helpful people around.

18. I don't want to bother them
Remember that you're offering something valuable; it's not a bother. This thought process is almost always exclusively in the head of the timid entrepreneur. Your potential clients do not see it as a bother; you follow up.

Chapter 7: Self-Belief and Selling

19. I can't sell
Change your self-perception and believe in your ability to sell. You could sell very well when you were a toddler. You can sell now.

20. I can make sales without selling
Active selling is vital for growing your business. Almost laughable. That's like saying I can swim without swimming. Or I can run without running. Or even I can breathe without breathing.

21. I'm going to outsource all of my selling
As the leader of your company, maintain a personal connection with your customers. Hear me clearly: the selling of your company's products and services cannot be completely outsourced! You too must contribute and sell as well.

Chapter 8: Words to Avoid in Sales

Sell or Sold
Although these are some of my personal favorite words, most people are much safer just not saying them in the presence of potential clients.

Example: "I sold the Joneses, I sold the Thompsons, I sold this to the Williams, we sell more than anyone else."

Replace with: Help or Helped.

Whenever tempted to say the word sell or sold, replace it with help or helped, and it fits beautifully every time!

Better Example: "I helped the Joneses, I helped the Thompsons, I helped the Williams, we have helped more than anyone else."

Sign or Signature
"I feel like I'm about to sign my life away." You've heard this expression before, and there's a reason why. Most people have, at one time or another, signed something they regret: a gym membership, a cell phone agreement…

something. So just the word spoken adds angst to the potential client.

Replace with:
- Autograph
- Your name
- Your approval
- Your John Hancock

Or any other way you like, just don't ask them to sign.

Contract
The word contract makes people feel locked in with no way out.

Replace with:
- The proposal
- The paperwork
- The agreement

Just don't use the word contract.

Price

If you offer a service, you do not have a price. Sweaters have a price, tires have a price, but your services are...

Replace with:
- Offered at…
- Made available for…
- Valued at…

Payment or Down Payment
Most people feel they already have enough payments, and they do not want any more from you!

Replace with:
- You offer terms to make it easier to pay for
- Initial investment or upfront money

The Worst Sentence to Say
"Since you agree to my price, all you have to do is sign the contract, give me a down payment, we will set up monthly payments for you, and we can consider this sale complete."

Instead, try something like:
"Since you see the value in our services, we can finalize the agreement with your approval,

arrange an initial investment, and set up terms that work best for you. We'll be on our way to helping you achieve your goals."

Chapter 9: Keywords to Use Much More Often

Understand this: people will buy from you or hire you for either emotional reasons or logical reasons.

Logical reasons stem from practicality—it makes sense or is a smart decision. Emotional reasons, however, arise when the potential client can imagine what it would feel like after the transaction is done. Logic relates to the Brain, while Emotion relates to the Heart. It is not worth arguing, but people buy much faster for emotional reasons than for logical reasons. Recognizing this, we must learn to use emotional words to sell!

The most emotional word in the English language starts with an L. Many adults have taught themselves not to say this word. The word is Love! I want you to use this word a lot more often and more comfortably.

Give me a sentence using the word Love to sell your services:

____

____

____

Now, if the sentence you wrote starts with "I love…" try again. Try it without 'you' being the star of the story. Start with "You're going to love…" or "My clients say they love…":

____

____

____

Use the second sentence.

The second most emotional word in English starts with an H: Home.

- "Home is where the heart is."
- "I'll be home for Christmas."
- "Home sweet home."

For most people, the word home has a very positive connotation. Home signifies security, comfort, and safety.

Give me a sentence using the word Home to sell your services:

____

____

____

Here are a few examples:
- "If you let me help you, everyone in your home will notice the benefits."
- "You will feel so much better going home knowing that _______ has been done for the day."

A sentence using both "home" and "love" with good voice tonality can have an almost hypnotic effect:
- “You are going to love going home knowing that _______.”

The next word I want you to use more often is the word most adults wish they heard more often: their own first name. Every time you say a person's name, you get a little more attention, almost like you are edifying them or complimenting them just by saying their name. The coolest thing about saying a person's name is that you cannot overdo it. You can say a person's name again and again, and they will like it each time!

The fourth word in this category is one I want you to use, but sparingly. This word has the power to change minds. It has worked on you all your life. The word is Because. Everything you say after "because" takes on more weight, power, and is believed more. "Because" indicates that there is more to the story coming

and has the power to change minds. For example:
- "I know what you said, but I want you to reconsider, because if you do change your mind, you will get these benefits sooner."

Learn the skillful use of these words: Love, Home, people's first names, and Because.

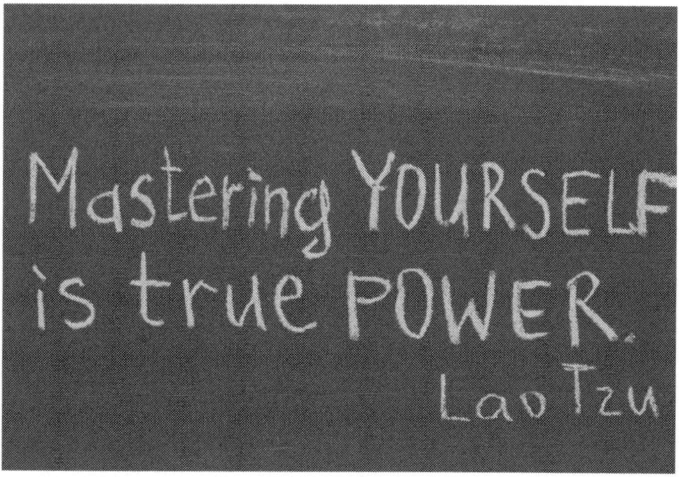

Mastering Sales Language: Conclusion

The journey to Mastering Sales Language is one of ongoing growth and self-awareness. As you've explored in this book, the words you choose to use — both in conversations with potential clients and in your own thoughts — hold significant power over your sales success. By eliminating the 21 harmful phrases outlined and embracing words that foster trust, value, and confidence, you're well on your way to becoming a more effective and persuasive entrepreneur.

Remember, sales is not about manipulation or pressure; it's about building genuine connections and helping others see the value in what you offer. When you shift your mindset from simply selling to genuinely helping, you create a positive experience for both you and your clients. This approach not only enhances your sales outcomes but also strengthens your integrity and reputation.

Here are a few key takeaways to keep in mind as you continue your sales journey:

1. Mindset Matters: Let go of limiting beliefs and embrace the identity of a confident, capable salesperson.
2. Value Communication: Clearly articulate the worth of your offerings and confidently address any misconceptions about affordability or need.
3. Customer-Centric Approach: Focus on building relationships and providing solutions, rather than pushing products.
4. Positive Language: Avoid words that create anxiety or resistance; instead, choose language that conveys ease, value, and partnership.
5. Continuous Improvement: Sales is a skill that can always be refined. Stay open to learning and adapting your approach.

By integrating these principles into your daily practice, you'll not only see a significant improvement in your sales performance but also in your overall satisfaction and confidence as an entrepreneur. Your words are powerful tools — use them wisely, and watch your business thrive.

Thank you for taking the time to read this book. Now, it's time to put these insights into action. Go forth and sell with enthusiasm, integrity, and the knowledge that you have the power to help your clients achieve their goals.

Here's to your continued success in mastering the language of sales!

About the Author

Brian K McNeill is a renowned Sales Confidence Coach and dynamic Sales Speaker, widely acclaimed for his transformative impact on individuals and businesses. With an illustrious career spanning decades, Brian has earned hundreds of glowing testimonials attesting to the effectiveness of his services.

Hailing from the vibrant streets of Brooklyn, New York, Brian brings a unique blend of street smarts and corporate savvy to his approach. Currently based in Charlotte, North Carolina, he operates as both a corporate Sales Trainer and an influential figure in the realm of sales education.

Brian is not only a captivating speaker but also a prolific author, having penned seven books that have become staples in the sales industry. His latest book, "Mastering Sales Language," joins the ranks of his celebrated works such as "The Shortcut!" and "Asking for the Money," reflecting his passion for empowering individuals to achieve unprecedented success in sales.

In his spare time, Brian indulges in two of his favorite hobbies: enjoying fine cigars and engaging in strategic battles on the chessboard. He finds solace and inspiration in these pursuits, which fuel his creativity and sharpen his strategic thinking.

Together with his wife, Brian embarks on exciting travels, enriching both his personal and professional experiences. With an unwavering commitment to excellence and a relentless drive to empower others, Brian K McNeill continues to make an indelible mark on the world of sales.

For more insight into Mastering Sales with Brian K. McNeill you may connect with him on all social media: @TheSalesConfidenceCoach.

Schedule your complimentary consult: calendly.com/bkmcneill

Access all books, audio books, webinars, and free downloads via: https://linktr.ee/thesalesconfidencecoach

Bibliography

Books

1. The Shortcut! The fastest route to selling your services better than you ever have before, so that you earn more money than ever before

2. Asking for the Money: How anyone can close more sales, even you

3. Why Rhinos Make Great Salespeople: featuring Mr. Randall the Rhino

4. Why Rhinos Make Great Entrepreneurs: featuring Mr. Randall the Rhino

5. 9 3 2: The 9 most important words, the three most important skills, and the two most important questions

6. Mastering Sales Language: eliminate these 21 harmful phrases and embrace words that Sell

Audiobooks

1. Asking for the Money: How anyone can close more sales, even you

2. 9 3 2: The 9 most important words, the three most important skills, and the two most important questions

Your Notes:

Your Notes:

Your Notes:

Made in the USA
Columbia, SC
12 July 2025

60366754R00026